DONALD DRIVER

A PACKER FOR LIFE

Copyright 2013 KCI Sports Publishing
All rights reserved. Unauthorized reproduction and distribution prohibited.

ISBN: 978-1-940056-00-5

Book layout & cover design: Nicky Brillowski

Printed in the United States of America
KCI Sports Publishing   3340 Whiting Avenue, Suite 5   Stevens Point, WI 54481
Phone: 1-800-697-3756   Fax: 715-344-2668
www.kcisports.com

Cover: Photography by Jim Biever
Photos: © Jim Biever, Michael Biever, Vernon Biever, reprinted with permission.

A PACKER FOR LIFE

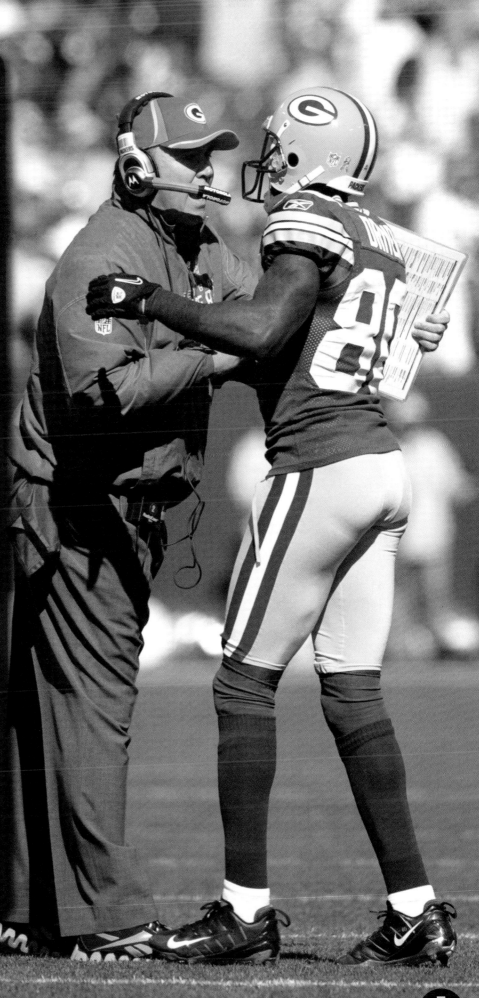

In a retirement ceremony filled with cheers and tears, there was no moment more powerful than McCarthy breaking down while telling a story of dinner with Driver and his family following the semifinals of "Dancing with the Stars."

"It's been said a couple times, the word 'special,' and I think that best describes Donald," McCarthy said. "The best part of the trip was Ruth's Chris Steakhouse afterwards. Lord knows what time we left there, but just to spend time with the family ..."

After regaining his composure, McCarthy continued: "I'm talking about the husband. I'm talking about the father. I'm talking about the friend. He's given a tremendous amount to our organization and will continue. Thank you, Donald. Thank you, Betina."

–Packers Coach Mike McCarthy

Driver breaks the tackle of the Vikings Henri Crockett (52). *Photo by Jim Biever*

Driver heads up field after a catch against San Diego in 2003. *Photo by Jim Biever*

Donald Driver. The very thought of his name conjures memories of that big smile and of Lambeau Leaps, of feet as graceful on the football field as on the dance floor.

Never is a long time, but it's safe to say there will never be another Donald Driver.

Never.

His is the ultimate rags-to-riches story. Sure, some other total nobody will emerge from some team's training camp and defy the odds with a spectacular career.

But nobody will ever do it like Driver.

Every player hates training camp. Driver smiled through practically every practice.

Chad Johnson celebrated with popcorn and pom-pons. Donald

Driver fights off Miami's Renaldo Hill (24) for extra yardage. *Photo by Jim Biever*

Driver celebrated by jumping into the seats.

Terrell Owens "loved me some me." Driver loved kids from ages 1 to 92.

Randy Moss mooned the fans. Driver retired in front of them.

Driver never forgot the game was a game and it was for the fans. He never griped about money or playing time. He became a pillar of the community as a spokesman for Goodwill and by taking over Brett Favre's charity softball game. He visited hospitals and signed auto-graphs. Inexplicably, a past-his-prime wide receiver won the nation's hearts en route to winning a dancing competition.

He set records. He won hearts. But perhaps most amazing of all, Driver was a man of his word.

Driver said he'd make Ron Wolf proud after the then-Packers general manager used a seventh-round draft pick on him in 1999.

He did.

It was early in his first training camp when Driver, a spindly

Driver has a friendly chat with the referee prior to a 2006 game in Cincinnati. *Photo by Jim Biever*

rookie receiver from Alcorn State who was mired near the bottom of the depth chart, spoke boldly at his locker. He wasn't cocky but he was confident.

"I've proved that I have great hands, and I have great speed and I have great jumping ability. So, I think those three greats should make for excellence," Driver said.

He was right.

Years later, Driver vowed he would never play for another team.

He didn't.

RAGS TO RICHES

Everyone loves an underdog, and there was no bigger underdog than Driver.

By now, you know the story by heart. Driver's parents divorced when he was a young boy and his father spent time in prison. Nights were spent in the back of a U-haul, and dinner sometimes consisted of mayonnaise or syrup sandwiches. When his mom, Faye Gray, would go to work the graveyard shift as a hotel security guard, Driver would run the streets. It wasn't the right thing to do, but drugs were sold and cars were stolen.

"The road I was going down as a kid, God found a way to get me out of it," Driver said. "I'm just blessed to be able to stand up here today and say I've reached all the milestones I can reach."

He reached them through sports. At Houston's Milby High School, Driver won 19 letters. It was enough to get him a scholarship at Alcorn State.

He reached them through love. Driver met his future wife, Betina Jackson, while at Alcorn State.

"Baby, I love you," an emotional Driver said, turning to Betina. "I thank you for the love, the support for the last 16 years of our life, the 14 years of playing this game and the 13 years of marriage. I've said it before, you're the back bone of our family. Life is what it is and life is whatever it may be, but life without you in my life is nothing. I love you."

At Alcorn State, Driver was an all-conference standout in track and field and football. In track

Driver is slammed to the turf by the Jaguars' Terry Cousin (21) during a 2007 game. *Photo by Jim Biever*

Driver looks for room to run against the Cowboys defense.   *Photo by Jim Biever*

and field, he competed in the high jump in hopes of qualifying for the 1996 Olympics. In football, he was coached by the man who mentored Jerry Rice, Johnny Thomas.

As a senior, Driver caught 55 passes and scored 10 touchdowns. That drew a young Packers scout named Alonzo Highsmith to the Lorman, Miss., campus.

"It was my first year scouting and Ron (Wolf) told me to go to Alcorn State, and I had no clue where Alcorn State was," Highsmith said. "From the immediate start, Donald Driver jumped out. He was enthusiastic, he was eager to go and I was impressed with his workout. I started talking to him more and I found out about some of his situations in life growing up and after that, I said, 'This kid is going to make it somewhere.' I didn't know how or where or what team he'd do it with, but I knew he was going to make it. "The person that came to mind that he reminded me of was my former college teammate, Michael Irvin. He reminded me of Michael, not in the football part, but just in the determination

13

and in the will to succeed and to overcome all odds, and I was impressed with him for that. I remember he came over to my car and said, 'Hey, I'm telling you, if you pick me, you won't be sorry.'"

Highsmith returned to Green Bay, where Wolf and the rest of the Packers' scouts – including future general manager Ted Thompson – turned on the film.

"When you see something special and when you see something different, (scouts will) say, 'Can you run that back?' Well, when we were doing Donald, we did that all the time," Thompson recalled. "We kept saying, 'Can you run that back? Can we see that again?' What we were seeing wasn't something you could define so much, it was just a special quality a player had. You could see not only his athletic ability, his ability to play the game, but through that grainy, black-and-white tape we had, you could see the enjoyment Donald had in playing the game. I think you could see the enjoyment Donald had playing the game throughout his entire career with the Packers."

As Wolf has joked in deflecting credit for unearthing this hidden

All eyes are on the coin flip prior to a game 2009 game in Arizona. *Photo by Jim Biever*

gem, if he were so smart for drafting Driver, he would have drafted him earlier. In fact, Wolf almost didn't draft Driver at all. Wolf hoped he could sign Driver as an undrafted free agent but, at High-smith's prodding, he took Driver with the Packers' 12th and final selection of the draft.

OH, REALLY?

"Packers load up on cornerbacks, neglect receiver need," read the Associated Press' headline.

Factually, the Packers didn't "neglect" their need at wide receiver. After all, they did draft Ohio State's Dee Miller in the sixth round as well as Driver in the seventh.

They were two of the 30 receivers taken in that draft and two of the dozen on the roster at the start of training camp. Before he was No. 80, Driver was No. 13, and he was No. 10 on the

Prior to getting his familiar #80 jersey, Driver was a little known rookie wearing #13. *Photo by Jim Biever*

Driver jumps over some pads during a drill at training camp.   *AP Photo*

depth chart. Antonio Freeman, Robert Brooks and Bill Schroeder were the established performers, Desmond Howard was a Super Bowl hero and Derrick Mayes a former second-round pick. Corey Bradford had flashed some potential as a fifth-round pick in 1998. A couple weeks before the 1999 draft, Jahine Arnold was acquired in a trade with Pittsburgh. Miller had the big-school pedigree. That left Driver fighting for snaps with first-year player Tyrone Goodson and undrafted rookies Zola Davis and Mike Vaughn.

Driver wasted no time in making his dash up the depth chart.

"I (can) remember specifically a play where we were in a red-zone drill and Donald was wearing No. 13 at the time," recalled coach Mike McCarthy, the team's quarterbacks coach in 1999. "Brett Favre was our quarterback and he threw this ball with the velocity

Above: Driver caught everything thrown his way during his first training camp in 1999. *AP Photo*

that it looked like it was going to go over the fence down there at Hinkle Field. Out of nowhere, here comes Donald Driver (who) makes a big catch. You could see right away this young man definitely belonged regardless of the seventh-round pick where he came from. You could see the smile, the athletic ability. It was a tremendous first impression I'll never forget."

Driver left a tremendous impression on star safety Darren Sharper, as well.

"My first memory of Donald was when he was the seventh-round pick in 1999 and we didn't know who he was," said Sharper, who played for the Packers from 1997 through 2004. "I remember a practice when he was a rookie and I was already a starter and I was covering him in the slot. I wasn't worried about him at all, and so when Brett threw the ball, it looked like it was thrown too far and I thought for sure it'd be an incompletion. Out of nowhere, Driver makes this flying, one-handed catch against me. It was incredible. In that training camp he just made play after play after play

Driver, right, has some fun with Noah Herron (23) during training camp in 2007.   *AP Photo*

and you could just tell that with how hard he worked and the skills that he had, he was just special."

Driver had to wait most of his rookie season to join Favre and Co. on the field.

The Packers' playoff hopes were crushed – as was the one-year reign of coach Ray Rhodes – when the plodding Carolina quarterback, Steve Beuerlein, beat the Packers with a 5-yard touchdown run on the game's final play at Lambeau Field on Dec. 12, 1999. Forgotten in history was Driver's first NFL catch.

Forced into action due to an injury, Driver scored an 8-yard touchdown to give the Packers the lead in the third quarter.

"It was the turning point of my career," Driver would say years later.

It wasn't an immediate turning point. Through three seasons, Driver caught just 37 passes. A restricted free agent following the 2001 season, Driver was courted by Kansas City but elected to stay in Green Bay. In 2002, Driver caught 70 passes for 1,064 yards and nine touchdowns.

Driver breaks away from Carolina Panthers' Deon Grant for a 31-yard touchdown pass from tight end Bubba Franks in 2002. *AP Photo*

STAR IS BORN

Driver made the first of his four Pro Bowls following that season. As the 213th selection of the 1999 draft, Larry McCarren (No. 308 in 1973) and Don Majkowski (No. 255 in 1987) are the only players in franchise history to be drafted later than Driver but selected to the Pro Bowl.

In November 2002, Driver was rewarded with the first of three contract extensions. It was then that Driver said he would play his entire career with the Packers.

For the next several years, Driver put up

Driver races away from the Browns' Chris Crocker in 2005.
Photo by Jim Biever

one monster season after another. He established team records with 743 receptions, 10,137 receiving yards and 133 consecutive games with a catch, smashing the old records held by Sterling Sharpe (595 receptions), James Lofton (9,656 yards) and Sharpe (103 consecutive games). He posted six consecutive seasons of 1,000 yards. Only Reggie Wayne matched that feat over the same period.

"I have great memories of playing with Donald," said Favre, Driver's quarterback for his first nine seasons. "He was a great teammate – he was very likable in the locker room. That he could go from a seventh-round draft choice to the Packers' all-time leading receiver is a real tribute to him."

Among receivers drafted in the seventh round or later or to go undrafted in NFL history, Driver ranks fifth in receptions.

"Throughout my career, Donald has been an incredible player and teammate whose durability and productivity speak for themselves," said Aaron Rodgers, Driver's quarterback for his final five seasons. "He was a huge part of helping me establish myself as a starter in this league and I'll always appreciate his encouragement and support during that time.

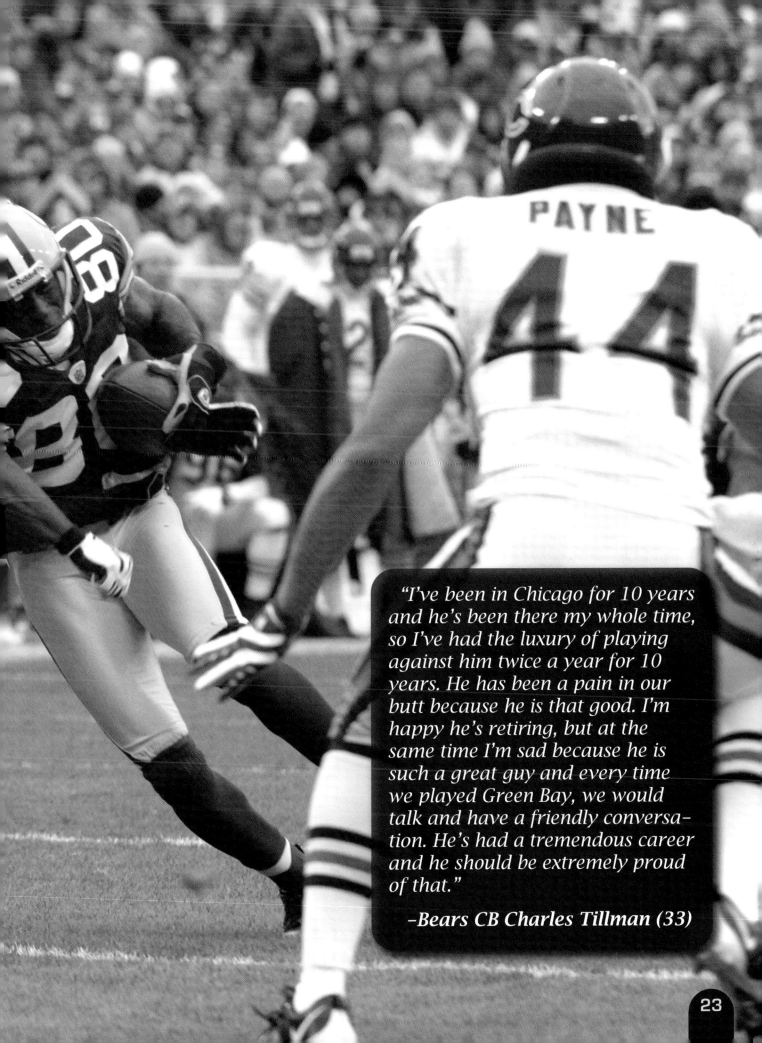

"I've been in Chicago for 10 years and he's been there my whole time, so I've had the luxury of playing against him twice a year for 10 years. He has been a pain in our butt because he is that good. I'm happy he's retiring, but at the same time I'm sad because he is such a great guy and every time we played Green Bay, we would talk and have a friendly conversation. He's had a tremendous career and he should be extremely proud of that."

—Bears CB Charles Tillman (33)

Driver goes down low to snare a pass as the Colts' Melvin Bullitt (33) closes in. *Photo by Jim Biever*

"More than (anything), I'll remember the attitude and professionalism that he carried himself with, especially in his approach to practice every day. I could count on one hand the number of practices he missed in my career, and his enthusiasm for the game always had such a positive impact on the rest of us. Donald was an awesome player, and an even better person who set a great example for giving back to the community."

Driver's numbers were great but some perspective brings additional luster.

Of the other 29 receivers selected in 1999, only Torry Holt produced better numbers with 920 receptions, 13,382 yards, 74 touchdowns and seven Pro Bowls. Other than that, only Marty Booker (539), Peerless Price (403) and Brandon Stokley (384) had one-half of Driver's reception total. Only eight had even one-fourth of Driver's total. A dozen of them didn't even catch 10 passes, including eight who were selected before Driver. Only Stokley was on the field in 2012.

"He is a very special individual," Wolf said. "It is rare in this game of

Driver runs through a tunnel of teammates prior to a 2005 game against Cleveland at Lambeau Field.   *Photo by Jim Biever*

professional football to come across a player whose dedication to the game and to the Green Bay Packers was always first and foremost in his individual makeup. When you think of all the great receivers that have played for the Packers, those magical names like (Don) Hutson, (James) Lofton, Sharpe and (Billy) Howton, there is only one who is the all-time leader in receptions and he is a seventh-round draft choice from Alcorn State University. That speaks volumes for his approach to this, the greatest game in American sports. He was a tough, hard-nosed individual who would go anywhere on the field in order to catch the football. He had the desire to excel, the ability to make it happen and the want-to to get it done. I personally am very proud of what Donald Driver has accomplished. He is a beacon for all those who want to because he did."

RESPECT

He did it through hard work.

This was no first-round pick who had the world handed to him on a silver platter since his high school days.

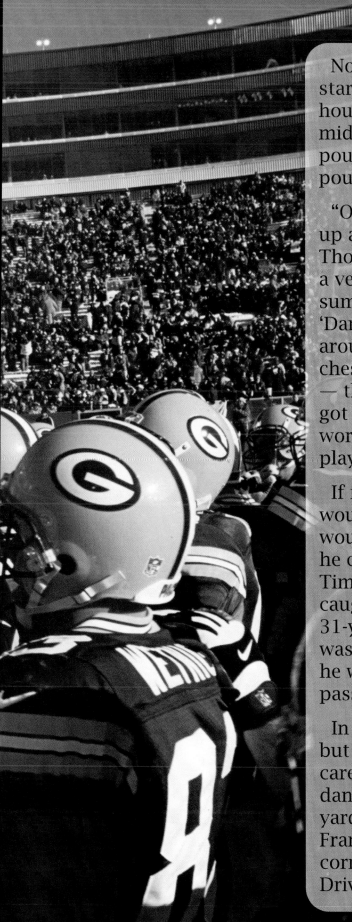

No, this is the story of a 175-pound track star building himself into a 194-powerhouse ready, willing and able to roam the middle of the field between menacing 250-pound linebackers and hard-charging 200-pound safeties.

"Our first minicamp (in 1999), he shows up and he's this skinny, skinny guy," Thompson recalled. "Good player, but he's a very skinny guy. He was nothing like this summer when you guys were watching 'Dancing with the Stars.' He's dancing around half-naked, all chiseled up, big chest, big shoulders, all that sort of stuff — that wasn't like he was when he first got here, but it is a credit to him and working hard. He kept playing and kept playing and kept playing, and he made it."

If it wasn't unlikely enough that Driver would carve out any sort of career, it would have been preposterous to believe he could outrun cornerbacks and Father Time for so long. A 30-year-old Driver caught 86 passes in 2005, 92 passes as a 31-year-old in 2006, 82 passes when he was a 32-year-old in 2007, 74 passes when he was a 33-year-old in 2008 and 70 passes when he was a 34-year-old in 2009.

In 2010, Driver caught "just" 51 passes but made the most remarkable play of his career. He showed the footwork of a dancer and the power of a fullback in a 61-yard touchdown for the ages against San Francisco. Poor Nate Clements: The Niners cornerback had three chances to bring Driver down but failed every time.

Team huddle prior to the start of a Christmas Eve game in 2000. *Photo by Jim Biever*

"When you're looking for a picture of what Donald Driver means to your football team, what he means as a player, that's the picture. That's the one I'll always remember," McCarthy said.

Like "Rocky" became a movie icon because he won as the ultimate underdog, Driver became more and more of a fan favorite as fans grew to appreciate his humble beginnings, his genuine smile and his unparalleled production.

Driver's role finally diminished but the love affair never faded. Rather, it intensified. It wasn't just the fans. He stepped aside with grace as Greg Jennings took over as the No. 1 receiver. He never complained as Jordy Nelson, James Jones and, later, Randall Cobb took his playing time.

Driver had a strong training camp this past summer but finished the season with only eight catches. He probably could have continued his career elsewhere for some receiver-starved team. But, a decade earlier, he had promised fans that he would never play for another team other than the Packers.

The world of sports is a graveyard of broken promises. Driver, however, stayed true to his words.

All good things must come to an end. This, however, was not the end of the story. Rather, you got the feeling that this was simply the end of one chapter and the beginning of the next. ■

December 12, 1999, vs. Carolina Panthers at Lambeau Field

The first catch of Driver's career was a memorable one. Running a "saddle cross route," Driver came free for an 8-yard touchdown from Brett Favre. The only part of the play Driver messed up was the celebration. "I remember when I scored, I didn't know what to do," recalled Driver years later. "Everyone was screaming, 'Go do the Leap! Go do the Leap!' And at that time, I kept asking them, 'What are you all talking about when you say the Leap.' I just did some dance and ran back to the sideline because I was so happy... I think that was the turning point of my career. Like, 'I can do this. I can play on this level and I'm good at it.' I think that moment, as well as when I got the phone call from Ron Wolf telling me I had made the team, that's when I felt like I had made it."

Driver catches his first pass as a Packer – an 8-yard touchdown. **Inset:** Favre congratulates the rookie Driver. *Photo by Jim Biever*

Driver high-fives Terry Glenn (83) during a 2002 game against Detroit. *Photo by Jim Biever*

Donald Driver was politely interrupted before he could even begin. Teammate Javon Walker, at his locker nearby, felt the need to speak up after overhearing a question from a reporter which basically went like this, "Donald, can you describe how good Javon has been this season?"

"Hey, if there wasn't a Driver," shot a candid Walker to the reporter, "this offense wouldn't be functioning at all thc positions."

Like Walker that 2004 season, receivers billed at the next great No. 1 passing option in Green Bay have come and gone since 1999. None have endured quite like Driver. In a sense, Driver has always been No. 1-receiver good without necessarily being labeled as such by outsiders.

"No one gives me credit for being a top receiver in the league and I've got to keep every year proving them wrong," said Driver at the Packers Hall of Fame banquet in 2006.

Starting from his first training camp in 1999, Driver's talent has always popped. But it took him some time in Green Bay to become entrenched in the lineup.

Driver first won a starting job coming out of training camp in 2002. Bill Schroeder, the Packers' leading receiver the season before had departed via free agency and veterans Antonio Freeman and Corey Bradford were also gone. That left an opening for a starter and Driver beat out Robert Ferguson, Charles Lee, and the rookie first-round draft pick, Walker, for the job.

The Packers also brought in Terry Glenn that season as their prize free agent. Glenn assumed the No. 1 receiver position in the off-season with all the departures. But when the pads came on, Driver stood out.

While Glenn had his moments, Driver emerged as one of the NFL's most explosive playmakers. He led the Packers with 70 catches, 1,064 receiving yards and nine touchdowns earning his first Pro Bowl selection. In the process, he had more catches in his first year as a starter than any of the top 10 wide receivers in Packers' history had in their initial season in the lineup.

Driver held on to his starting spot for 10 consecutive seasons and was remarkably durable for his slight, but sturdy frame. He missed just two games during that span due to injury.

As other receivers — the afore-mentioned Glenn and Walker and

Javon Walker, Donald Driver, Antonio Freeman, Robert Ferguson. Photo by Jim Biever

Driver discusses a route with quarterback Brett Favre during a 2002 game at Minnesota.
Photo by Jim Biever

even Greg Jennings — assumed or were being anointed the No. 1 receiver during Driver's career, Driver led the team in receiving six times. In 2005, he had 37 more catches than the next closest wide receiver on the Packers roster. In 2006, he had 47 more. And in 2007, he had 29 more.

Said Favre during Driver's 82-catch season in 2007, "Donald, I hate to say quietly, has done his job. I don't know how you can say quietly or how anyone can look past what that guy has done. (He) has not been mentioned as one of the top receivers in this league, but what separates him is he shows up every day, works hard, keeps his mouth shut. He's a playmaker. I think that's an understatement."

In 2004, Driver and Walker gave Favre his most productive wide receiver tandem ever. With 173 catches, 2,590 receiving yards and 21 touchdowns, the duo became the

Donald Driver & Javon Walker – the most prolific wide receiving duo in Packers history.
Photo by Jim Biever

Walker & Driver in 2004
173 catches
2,590 receiving yards
21 touchdowns

most prolific in any one season in Packers history. Walker led the team with 89 catches for 1,382 yards and 12 touchdowns but was quick to credit Driver for his success.

"You're only as good as your counterpart," said Walker that season. "If another receiver on the other side of you gets 100 yards, then it's a compliment to the other receiver. You remember a couple of years ago when (the Bills') Eric Moulds and Peerless Price both went over 1,000 yards? Then they split them both up? What has Peerless Price done since then? You're only as good as your counterpart, but I think the difference between us two and them, if you put us in an offense where if we didn't have each other anymore, we can still make something happen. But it only makes us better with us both being here."

A year later, with Walker sidelined with an ACL injury, Driver caught 86 passes and posted a career-best five 100-yard receiving games. A year after that, with Walker traded and head coach Mike McCarthy aboard for his first season, Driver set career marks with 92 catches and 1,295 yards (both fifth in the NFL that season). ■

The Packers' career leader in passing, Brett Favre, was acquired in 1992 with a first-round draft pick.

The Packers' career leader in rushing, Jim Taylor, was a second-round draft pick in 1958.

The Packers' career leader in tackles, John Anderson, was a first-round pick in 1978.

The Packers' career leader in interceptions, Bobby Dillon, was a third-round pick in 1952.

The Packers career leader in receptions — a record set by Donald Driver — was a seventh-round pick in 1999. The man whose record he broke, Sterling Sharpe, was a first-round pick in 1988. No. 3 on the Packers' list, James Lofton, was a first-round pick in 1978.

"There have been some great guys that played here before me, and to be mentioned in the same breath as those guys, it's an honor," Driver said while clutching the record-setting ball. "And now, when I leave, I told Bob Harlan a long time ago and Ron Wolf, if I never make it to Canton, Ohio, as long as I'm in the Packers Hall of Fame, that's all that matters to me."

Left: Driver with the reception that sets the career record. **Above:** Driver salutes the crowd after his record-setting catch. *Photos by Jim Biever*

Photo by Jim Biever

As if there was any doubt about Driver's Packers Hall of Fame credentials, he solidified himself with a typically sublime performance on Sunday against Detroit. Needing one catch to break a tie with Sharpe, Driver got it in the first quarter. He tacked on six more along the way to give him 602 for his career.

"Oh, is that what I've got? Oh, yeah, that is good," Driver said. "I guess if I can get to 1,000, that'd be great, wouldn't it? I've got a long way to go, so I'll take the 600 right now."

Driver set the record on a quick-hitting pass to the left sideline that gained 5 yards. After the play, Driver was congratulated by quarterback Aaron Rodgers and running back Ryan Grant, among others.

""Thank you,'" Rodgers recalled Driver telling him. "I'm the one thanking him for those big plays he's made for us."

"What a significant thing for him," linebacker Aaron Kampman said, "and just so happy for him to do it at home and I can't say enough about the professional that he is, the friend he is and the teammate he is. I'm very, very happy for him."

"I can't say enough about Donald Driver," coach Mike McCarthy said. "It couldn't happen to a finer individual. He's an outstanding representative of the Green Bay Packers. I'm very happy to be a part of that. I just can't say enough about him personally or professionally what he accomplished here today."

After the drive, which ended in a touchdown and a 14-0 lead, the congratulations and hugs and high-fives continued on the sideline.

"We're a family. Guys were really happy for me," Driver said. "Everybody was saying, 'Get the ball to him so he can get the record.' Once I got the record and got to the sidelines, so many guys were hugging

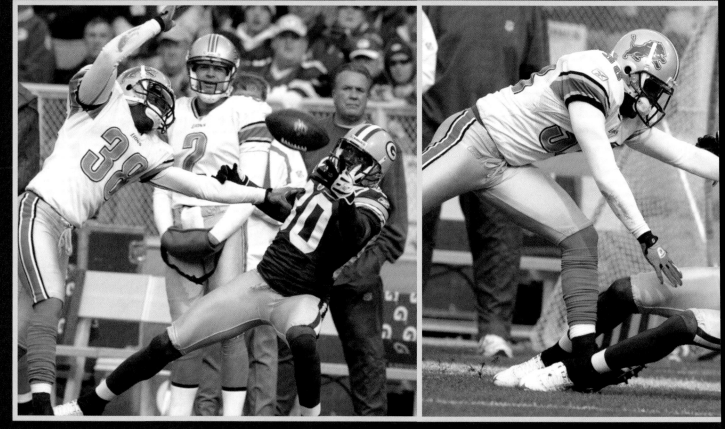

Driver makes an incredible catch despite being held and grabbed by the Lions' Demarcus Faggans.
Photos by Jim Biever

me and giving me congratulations. It was a real special moment. That is when you can't do anything but smile. Today is a real special day for me in my career."

Not bad for the 213rd selection of the 1999 draft. The wide receiver taken exactly 200 picks earlier, Troy Edwards, is a mere footnote in Steelers history. Not bad for the 26th of 31 receivers taken in the draft. Not bad for No. 13 on the 13-man receiving depth chart during his first training camp. Not bad who was an afterthought about rookie receivers — the Packers used a sixth-rounder on Dee Miller from big-name Ohio State. Not bad for a guy who had 37 catches total in his first three seasons.

"I am happy. I am very excited. It's a long time coming," Driver said. "You never expect it to happen, but it couldn't it come in a better place — at home in front of the fans I've played in front of for so many years. It feels good. Now, I just have to wait on Sterling to call me and congratulate me."

Driver's last catch was about as good as any he has made in his rags-to-riches career. While being held and grabbed by cornerback Demarcus Faggans on a deep route up the left sideline in the third quarter, Driver made a falling-down, one-handed catch. It was a near-replay of the catch he made a few weeks ago at St. Louis.

"James Jones had said that St. Louis catch was luck," Driver said. "After I caught this one today, he said maybe it is just one of those things where you can catch with one hand. I just concentrated on the ball and was able to bring it in. The defender was hanging on my other arm so I was just trying to do the best I can to get to the ball. After I made that catch, the crowd got really juiced up. It was a lot of fun."

With seven catches for 107 yards, Driver ran his season totals to 25 receptions for 395 yards. That puts him on pace for 80 catches for 1,264 yards. He's had more yards only once in his career, 2006, when he tallied 1,295 yards.

For added perspective, Driver is one of four Pro Bowl receivers from the Class of 1999 — first-rounders Torry Holt (seven Pro Bowls) and David Boston (one) and third-rounder Marty Booker (one) are the others. Three receivers were taken in the first round of that draft, with Driver's receptions total 84 more than Boston (No. 8 over-all) and Edwards (No. 13) combined.

Both James Jones and Greg Jennings joked that they'll be gunning for Driver's record, with Jones saying he's looking forward to that congratulatory call from Driver when the time comes. But considering the way the 34-year-old Driver is playing, who knows how many catches he'll wind up with.

Player	Receptions
1. Donald Driver, 1999-2012	743
2. Sterling Sharpe, 1988-94	595
3. James Lofton, 1978-86	530

"It is going to take them awhile," said Driver, who ranks second in team history with 8,384 receiving yards, 1,292 behind Lofton. "I am not done playing yet and I'm going to keep adding catches. When they finally run me out of here, then maybe they can take a run at it. As long as I'm here and they're here, it is going to be a battle."

With football in hand, Driver was looking forward to going home. Before leaving on Sunday morning, he was reminded by his son, Cristian, that he needed one catch to break the record.

"It's even more special because it came with a win," Driver said. "I don't think it would have felt this good if we would have lost the game. It feels good. The good thing about it was my son told me before I left the house that I had one more catch to make for the record. I am happy I can go home and celebrate with them now."■

Driver dives in for a touchdown during 2nd quarter action against Tennessee in 2008. *Photo by Jim Biever*

August 21, 2000
Preseason at Miami

Though Driver made the Packers roster as a long-shot rookie in 1999, he was far from a lock entering 2000 under new head coach Mike Sherman. But an exciting 80-yard catch-and-run for a touchdown against the Dolphins helped answer any questions. "I think that was the big decision, the biggest factor in making the team," said Driver later that season. "There were a lot of guys – young guys, rookie receivers – in camp then and I think that catch probably let myself stand out in front of a lot of coaches... the game was on Monday Night Football. So it was like everybody across the world was watching it. Everybody remembers that 80-yarder by Green Bay."

Head coach Mike Sherman congratulates Driver as he comes off the field after scoring on a 80-yard touchdown. *Photo by Jim Biever*

Quarterback Aaron Rodgers congratulates Driver after scoring against the San Francisco 49ers in 2010. *AP Photo*

"It makes me really happy to know that Donald Driver is retiring as a Packer. Throughout my career, Donald has been an incredible player and teammate whose durability and productivity speak for themselves. He was a huge part of helping me establish myself as a starter in this league and I'll always appreciate his encouragement and support during that time. I'll remember all the great plays he made in our time together, including the long touchdown against San Francisco in 2010 that is still one of the most remarkable plays I've ever seen. He was one of the guys I was most happy for at the end of that season, because he had waited his whole career to get to the Super Bowl and win a ring. But more than any of those things, I'll remember the attitude and professionalism that he carried himself with, especially in his approach to practice every day. I could count on one hand the number of practices he missed in my career, and his enthusiasm for the game always had such a positive impact on the rest of us. Donald was an awesome player, and an even better person who set a great example for giving back to the community. I wish him the best in his next chapter and feel lucky that I got to share part of my career as his teammate."

–Packers QB Aaron Rodgers

Photo by Jim Biever

DD AND HIS KICKSTAND

As a child, Donald Driver was given the nickname "Quickie" in part because he was so difficult to keep up with. As an adult on the football field, the same elusiveness applied.

During his 14-year playing career, no one, pound-for-pound, was more difficult to bring down than Driver, who came to Green Bay with just 175 pounds on his 6-foot frame.

"He made a career out of going across the middle and making all the tough catches that needed to be made," said Driver's teammate of 11 years, Mark Tauscher.

As he grew in his career, Driver proved to be more than just a fast receiver with world-class leaping ability. He also became a dependable slot receiver willing to get the tough yards to keep the chains moving.

While yards-after-the-catch (YAC) is more of a mainstream statistic now, it was far from that during Driver's early years. Still, his first quarterback in the NFL found another term to describe Driver's unique after-the-catch ability.

After connecting with Driver on 10 passes for 114 yards in a 2005 game at Atlanta, Brett Favre said this about Driver's moves to get free from would-be tacklers: "They were joking on the sidelines saying Donald has a kickstand. He doesn't go down.

Driver catches his breath after taking a hard hit across the middle against Arizona in 2000. *Photo by Jim Biever*

Driver plants the "kickstand" and makes the Raiders' Anthony Dorsett (33) miss. *Photo by Jim Biever*

Guys grab him and he puts his kickstand down and pops out the other side. The guy's a tremendous athlete, very determined."

More than anything else, the "kickstand" became Driver's trademark move. The plant-and-pop reaction used for quick change of direction fooled countless defenders, sometime multiple ones on the same play.

A 61-yard touchdown in a 2010 game at Lambeau Field against the 49ers – which many have called the most memorable play of Driver's career – featured several mini-kick-stands which allowed Driver to zigzag his way to the end zone. Driver forced at least three missed tackles on the play racking up 38 yards after the catch.

"It was one of the most amazing catch and runs I've ever seen," said quarterback Aaron Rodgers.

Even into his mid-30's Driver remained a slippery receiver. One website that tracks such statistics had Driver among the top 14 receivers in the league in missed tackles each season from 2008-2010.

At Alcorn State, Driver posted a career average of 22.0 yards per catch including a 26.5 mark during his junior season in 1997. Those numbers were indicative of a rare player albeit on a smaller stage when current Packers general manager Ted Thompson was working under Ron Wolf preparing for the NFL Draft in 1999.

"You go through and you watch tape, and there's always – when you see something special and when you see something different in scout in the room and anybody can do it, they'll say, 'Can you run that back?'," said Thompson. "Well, when we were doing Donald, we did that all the time. We kept saying, 'Can you run that back? Can we see that again?' What we were seeing wasn't something you could define so much, it was just a special quality a player had. You could see not only his athletic ability, his ability to play the game, but through that grainy, black-

Driver lets fans know it is another Packers first down.
Photo by Jim Biever

Quarterback Brett Favre carries Driver off the field after a 68-yard touchdown pass against San Francisco in 2006.
Photo by Jim Biever

and-white tape we had from Alcorn A&M, you could see the enjoyment Donald had in playing the game. I think you could see the enjoyment Donald had playing the game throughout his entire career with the Packers."

Driver averaged over 15 yards per catch in three different seasons with the Packers. But Favre remembers him as a never-give-up receiver.

"Even though some of the big plays we had together come to mind – on Monday night in Champaign (Illinois), against the Giants in the playoffs – it really is the way he could make guys miss that stands out to me, like the long touchdown he had just before halftime in Minnesota (an 82-yarder in 2006)."

In a way, "Quickie" never grew up. From his childhood to the football field and even on the dance floor, he has always been a jitterbug.

Perhaps Favre said it best at a 2007 press conference: "You could put Donald in a phone booth with 11 guys and it'll take 'em five minutes to touch him."■

December 30, 2001, vs. Minnesota Vikings at Lambeau Field

Lost among Driver's 64 career touch-downs receptions (including the post-season) was his lone rushing touchdown, a 31-yard score on a reverse. Adding to the excitement of the play was a key block by none other than quarterback Brett Favre.

Right: The temperature at kickoff was 19 with a 14-mph northwest wind that dropped the wind chill to 5.
Photo by Jim Biever

Opposite Page: Bubba Franks (88) and Corey Bradford (85) congratulate Donald Driver after scoring a touchdown on a 31-yard reverse.
AP Photo

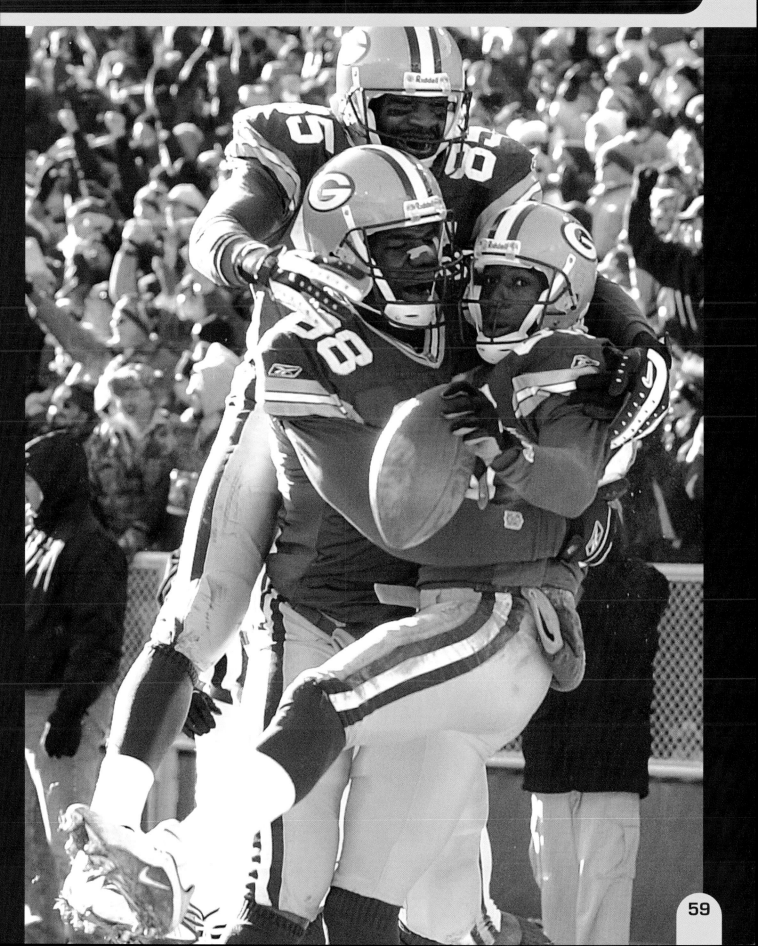

Driver is tackled by Carolina Panthers' Captain Munnerlyn (41) during the second game of the 2011 season. The 10-yard reception allowed Driver to break the franchise receiving yards record previously held by James Lofton.
AP Photo

DD RECEIVING YARDS

Driver with James Lofton. *Photo by Jim Biever*

The immortal Don Hutson will forever serve as the gold standard for receivers in Packers history.

Who's No. 2? No. 80, of course.

In 2003, James Lofton was inducted into the Pro Football Hall of Fame. His 14,004 career receiving yards rank eighth in NFL history. Of those, his 9,656 yards during nine seasons in Green Bay stood as the franchise record until another No. 80 came along.

After a quiet first three seasons in the league, Driver topped 1,000 yards in seven of his next eight seasons. Finally, during the second game of the 2011 season, Driver broke Lofton's record at Carolina.

"I hate to say it, that it's an honor when somebody breaks your record, but it kind of is," Lofton said. "He's a

Player	Receiving Yards
1. Donald Driver, 1999-2012	10,137
2. James Lofton, 1978-86	9,656
3. Sterling Sharpe, 1988-94	8,134

Driver hangs on for a 47-yard completion against Carolina in 2007. *Photo by Jim Biever*

real workmanlike receiver. I think if kids are watching the game today, he's the type of player that you'd want to emulate and you'd point to and say, 'You want to play like this guy does.' I'm really proud of him because he wasn't a high draft pick. He's built himself into a receiver who can take a lot of hits but also a guy that's really good after the catch. He's just a strong, physical presence. He's obviously played with some good quarterbacks but at the same time he's made them look good."

"I think when you have goals, you want to achieve them all," Driver said. "When I got closer to the individual receiving records, I wanted them. When I didn't have them and I was far away, it never crossed my mind. When I got closer to consecutive games (with a catch), Sterling held that record for a long time, I wanted it. When I got close to receptions, Sterling held it, I wanted it. When I got closer to the yards, James held it, I wanted it. Once I broke that, where do I go from there? It's just set my legacy to where my name one day gets in the rings and I get in the Packers Hall of Fame and then my jersey gets retired. I may one day be lucky enough to get that wish. If I don't, when someone else wears 80, I hope he carries the number like I did for James Lofton." ■

#80 GREATEST MOMENT

October 7, 2002 vs. Chicago Bears at Champaign, Illinois

On the Monday Night Football stage, but in an unfamiliar setting, Brett Favre and Driver hooked up for their longest regular season touchdown together, an 85-yard play on a rainbow of a pass. In a game played in Champaign on the campus of the University of Illinois due to the renovation of Soldier Field, Driver not only had the first 100-yard receiving game of his career, but also the attention of the football-watching nation.

Right: Driver catches a touchdown pass from quarterback Brett Favre for the Packers first score against the Chicago Bears during the first quarter of their Monday night game at Memorial Stadium in Champaign, IL, during the 2002 season. *AP Photo*

Opposite Page: Driver finished with 4 catches for 120 yards in the Packers 34-21 win. *Photo by Jim Biever*

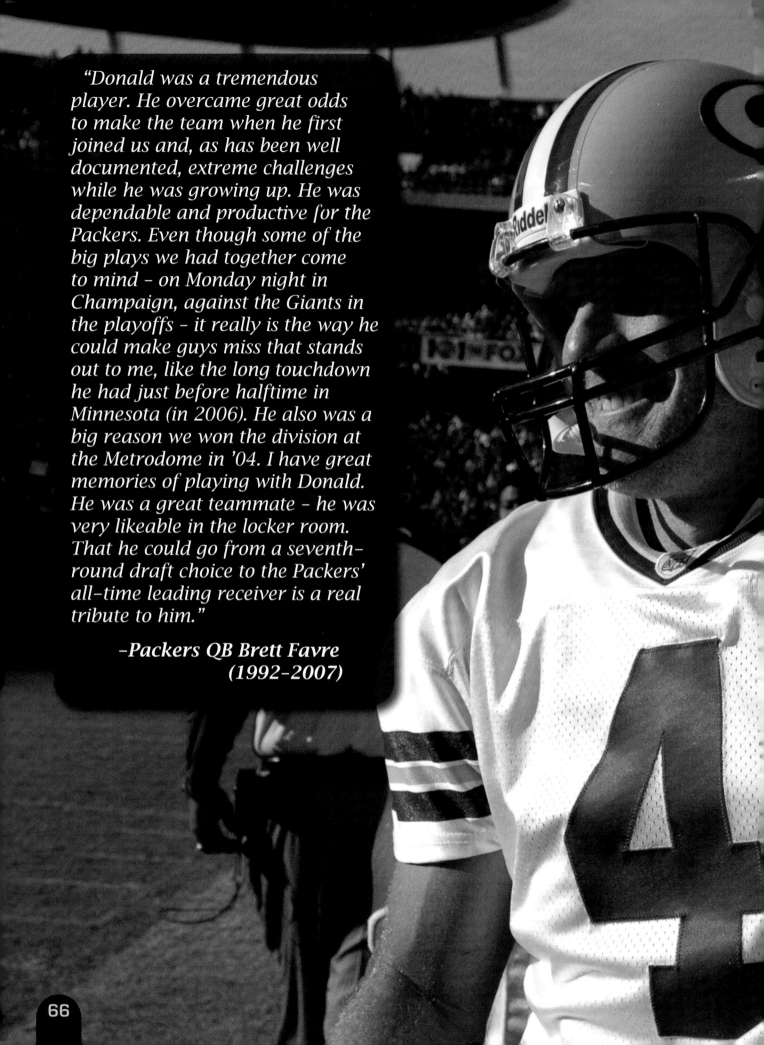

"Donald was a tremendous player. He overcame great odds to make the team when he first joined us and, as has been well documented, extreme challenges while he was growing up. He was dependable and productive for the Packers. Even though some of the big plays we had together come to mind – on Monday night in Champaign, against the Giants in the playoffs – it really is the way he could make guys miss that stands out to me, like the long touchdown he had just before halftime in Minnesota (in 2006). He also was a big reason we won the division at the Metrodome in '04. I have great memories of playing with Donald. He was a great teammate – he was very likeable in the locker room. That he could go from a seventh-round draft choice to the Packers' all-time leading receiver is a real tribute to him."

–Packers QB Brett Favre (1992–2007)

Aaron Kampman #74, Chad Clifton #76, Donald Driver #80, and Al Harris #31 take the field during pregame player introductions at the 2008 NFL Pro Bowl.   *AP Photo*

DD A PRO BOWL PLAYER

D onald Driver was selected to four Pro Bowls during his remarkable career. Only James Lofton (seven) and Sterling Sharpe (five) were picked for more among Packers receivers.

Driver picks up extra yardage after the catch during the second quarter of the 2008 Pro Bowl.
AP Photo

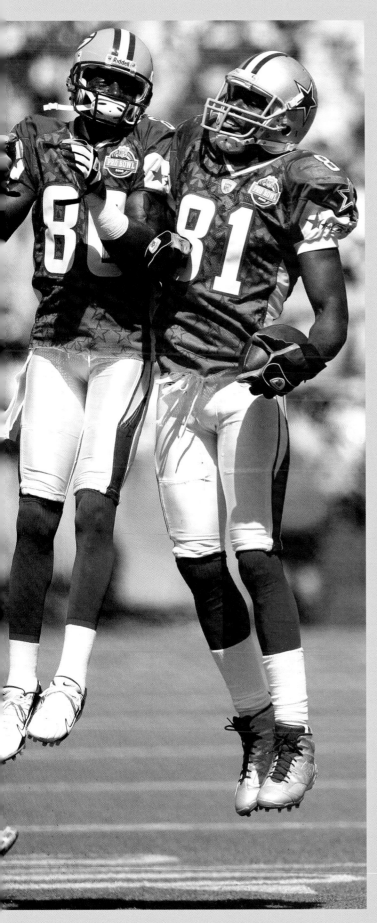

Terrell Owens (81) gets some air as he celebrates a hip bump with Driver after scoring a touchdown at the 2008 Pro Bowl. *AP Photo*

When Driver was named to his first Pro Bowl team following the 2002 season, he joined some other exclusive company. Only Larry McCarren (12th round) and Don Majkowski (10th round) were drafted later than Driver (seventh round) and selected to the annual all-star game.

Driver was an injury replacement in 2002, when he had his breakout season of 70 catches, 1,064 yards and nine touchdowns. All three stats eclipsed his totals from his first three seasons. He caught one pass for 9 yards in the game.

He was voted in for the first time in 2006, when he posted 92 catches, 1,295 yards and eight touchdowns. He caught three passes for 38 yards in the game.

"The last two years I felt like I should have went," Driver said when his selection was announced. "Last year, I was hoping I would get in. ... I was kind of doubting that I wasn't going to make it. You never know what is going to happen. It's basically politics."

He got the nod again in 2007, when he caught 82 passes for 1,048 yards and two touchdowns despite sitting out the regular-season finale. With Mike McCarthy coaching the NFC team, Driver caught two passes for 31 yards.

Driver was an alternate in 2010 and would have played in the game had the Packers not played in the Super Bowl.■

VE US TO XLII

King for a day.

That is what Donald Driver had to be thinking on Feb. 6, 2013, the day he officially announced his retirement from the Packers and the NFL. In a grand ceremony at the Lambeau Field Atrium that included a dedication, a key to the city of Green Bay, a street sign with his name, and appearances from local political figures, Driver ruled the world.

But the day, with its royal and cheerful feel, was about one thing at its core – the connection between the fans and their hero.

"This is the first time in Packers' history that we've had a public retirement of one of our players in front of the fans," said Packers president and CEO Mark Murphy.

Few in recent history for the Packers can match the draw of Driver. So when he decided to walk away from the game, he wanted his fans to be there to celebrate.

The week prior, free tickets were made available to the public to see Driver say good-bye. They were gone in 15 minutes. On the day of the event, some waited in line outside for hours in sub-freezing temperatures just to get a good spot, the best spot to view a Titletown legend.

Over 1,000 fans were eventually let in, standing behind a barricade that separated them from the media, Driver's family and friends, and special guests. But in reality, they had never been closer to Driver's heart.

"I told myself that I wasn't going to cry today so I'm going to try to hold all the emotions back as much as possible," Driver told a boisterous crowd in his opening comments. "But I have to say this, that I love you all so

Driver was a favorite of young Packer fans on the bike brigade at training camp. *Photo by Jim Biever*

much. You guys stood out in the cold to get tickets to share this moment with me. You all are crazy. But now you know why Packer fans are so special because they show the loyalty. They show the respect. So now, I give you all the respect."

Though it seems counter-intuitive, Driver's popularity grew later in his career even as his playing time diminished. By 2011, at 36 years old, he was really a starter on paper only. But his status as a Super Bowl champion put a cherry on his career, and winning ABC's hit show "Dancing With The Stars" gave him a boost, too, not only around the country, but also in the local community.

Driver has always accommodated his fans at every chance he got. From autograph sessions, to appearances for his children's books, to carrying on the tradition of a charity softball game from his old quarterback Brett Favre, he answered the call.

He listened intently to his fans, too, unlike that of most in his position. Upon his retirement, after seeing

Driver always made time for the fans no matter how young they were. *Photo by Jim Biever*

a news story of a 78-year old lady in Green Bay who just wanted a hug from Driver before he left town, Driver showed up at her door and delivered that hug. When he threw his cleats into the crowd at his charity softball game and an adult lady ripped them away from a young boy, Driver later met the boy and made his day. And when he got a letter from a fan early in his career regarding an out-of-character touchdown celebration with Robert Ferguson, Driver made sure it never happened again.

From there, Lambeau Leaps were

about the extent of his post-touchdown routine (with one exception in 2012 to honor his Dancing with the Stars triumph). By the end of his career, he was the franchise's all-time leader in receptions (743) and receiving yards (10,137) among an elite group of wide receivers including Sterling Sharpe, James Lofton, and one of the greatest ever, Don Hutson.

Like Hutson, Driver has Packers' receiving records. He has longevity, too. And a Super Bowl

Driver with the Lambeau Leap.   *Photo by Jim Biever*

championship puts him in a class with other Packers greats.

No one, however, will ever claim more popularity as a Packer. In the end, that was the lasting image of "a king" for a day. ∎

November 21, 2004
at Houston

Returning to play in his hometown for the first time, Driver blitzed the Texans with 10 catches for 148 yards. He had a 15-yard catch to set up a game-tying field goal and a 12-yard catch to set up the winning kick in overtime. The victory was the fifth straight for the Packers during a six-game streak.

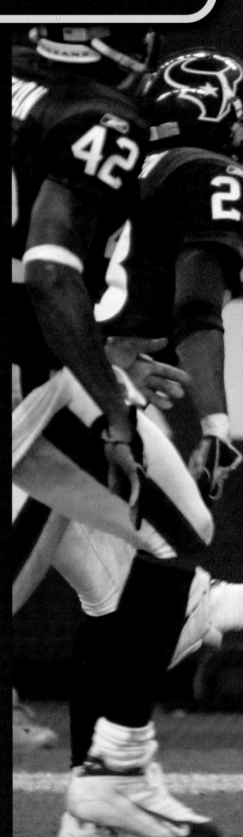

Above: Driver snares one of his 10 catches against the Texans. *Photo by Jim Biever*

Right: Driver reaches for a 24-yard touchdown catch as Texans' Dunta Robinson (23) and Marcus Coleman (42) defend during fourth quarter action. *AP Photo*

"A few things come to mind when I think about Donald. The first is the way he grew up and the hardships he had to endure early on in his life. Second is that he is one of the toughest competitors I have ever been around. And the third is how much the Green Bay community meant to him and how much he meant to Green Bay. With that said, I'll sum Donald up in three words: warrior, champion, friend!"

–Packers DB
Charles Woodson

Driver celebrates with the fans at Austin Straubel Airport after beating the Chicago Bears 21-14 in the NFC Championship. *AP Photo*

Driver answers questions during a pre-Super Bowl news conference in Irving, TX.   *AP Photo*

No one player on the Packers roster had waited longer. And no one among the assembled masses on this particular night – based on the spike in noise level – wanted anyone else to win it more than this guy.

Tiny Austin Straubel Airport in Green Bay, normally docile in its daily activity, was alive. The Packers were coming home just hours after winning the NFC Championship in Chicago to advance to the Super Bowl.

Hundreds formed a long, narrow walkway inside the terminal. When the Packers finally entered, the adoring fans began to cheer wildly.

Driver prepares for practice leading up to Super Bowl XLV against Pittsburgh. *AP Photo*

Driver, right, tosses a football as the Packers players and coaches arrive to a ball room for their final Super Bowl XLV walk through. *AP Photo*

The noise level remained constant until about five minutes into the procession of team officials, coaches and players. Then it reached a fever pitch. Donald Driver, grinning from ear-to-ear, was walking through.

In his 12th year in the NFL, having been to the playoffs seven times, Driver would finally play in the Super Bowl.

"To me, it means everything," said Driver a day later. "I think when you're playing in this league a long time, that is the ultimate goal to get to the Super Bowl, and then the ultimate goal after that is to win it. I'm excited about it. Like I said before, it hasn't hit me yet, but I know it will hit me soon that now I have the opportunity to go to the dance. The biggest thing for me now is to put that ring on my finger and be part of my legacy that I've been to the Super Bowl and I've also won the Super Bowl."

Though other Packers veterans on the 2010

team had similarly long waits for a Super Bowl – Chad Clifton and Mark Tauscher (11 years), Ryan Pickett (9 years to get back) and Charles Woodson (8 years to get back) – Driver was the clearly the sentimental favorite. Still going strong at 36, he was the only one on the roster dating back to head coach Ray Rhodes in 1999.

Driver played in 12 playoff games prior to the Super Bowl triumph. The only other time he really sniffed a Super Bowl was in 2007 when the Packers were upset by the Giants at Lambeau Field in the NFC Championship game. Driver sat on the bench after that game with a dejected stare wondering if he would ever get another shot while the Giants celebrated.

"I think you get to a point where it's hard to get here, and once you get in, then you just say 'Hey, I've got to win it all,'" said Driver leading up to the Super Bowl. "I don't think we had any doubt that we couldn't get here at all. One thing we did do is we believed. We believed that no one

Driver talks with the media prior to Super Bowl XLV. *AP Photo*

Win or lose Driver always made time for the fans. *Photo by Jim Biever*

could stop us. It started in March, and the crazy part about it is once we got to training camp, I think guys really believed in it. We started putting Super Bowl everywhere, and now we can say we're in it."

Driver started 15 games for the Packers in 2010 and recorded his franchise-record ninth season with 50 catches or more. He added 14 more catches in the playoffs. He also earned his fourth Pro Bowl selection.

But at least one teammate that season saw more than records and statistics.

"He means a lot not only to this team but to this organization," said fellow wide receiver Greg Jennings. "What he brings to the table is unmatched. You can't supplement for a guy like that. You can't take a piece like that out and kind of just plug a piece in. His veteran leadership, his game smarts, his football IQ. I mean, all of those intangibles, they're hard to imitate. They're hard to duplicate. And with a guy like that, I'm just fortunate he's in our room having not been afforded this opportunity to play on this stage." ■

December 24, 2004
at Minnesota

Driver came up big when the Packers needed it the most. After a 1-4 start to the season, the Packers clinched the NFC North Division on Christmas Eve at the Metrodome in one of the biggest regular season wins of the Mike Sherman era. Driver tied his career-high with 11 catches including a tough 3-yard touchdown reception (on a fourth-and-3) that tied the game at 31 in the fourth quarter.

Above: Driver looks for running room against the Vikings' Brian Russell (27). *Photo by Jim Biever*

Right: Driver dunks the football over the goalpost after scoring in the fourth quarter. *Photo by Jim Biever*

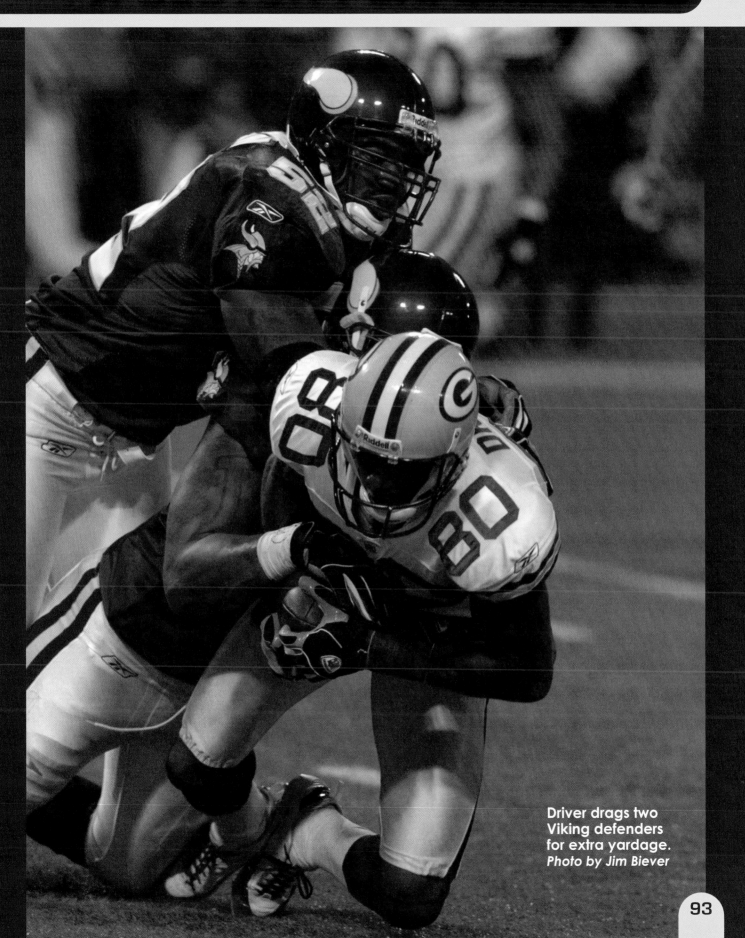

Driver drags two Viking defenders for extra yardage.
Photo by Jim Biever

Driver hauls in a 24-yard reception against the Steelers in Super Bowl XLV. *AP Photo*

With a towel wrapped around his neck, a walking boot on his foot, and cameras in his face, Donald Driver stood alone on the sideline, the moment having hit him whole-heartedly.

Tearing up, he wore a new hat that said it all: SUPER BOWL CHAMPIONS.

Just minutes earlier the Green Bay Packers had clinched Super Bowl XLV with a fourth-down stop on defense. Now, as the seconds ticked away on the game clock at Cowboys Stadium, Driver, after 12 years in the NFL, had reached the pinnacle of his playing career.

"If you had to pick one (highlight), I would say the moment I ran out that tunnel at the Super Bowl. That's a moment I'll never forget," said a reflective Driver on Feb. 6, 2013, the day of his official retirement announcement. "That's one memory – as an NFL player, we always say that's the greatest milestone is to make it to the National Football League and win a Super Bowl ring. I'll never forget that moment running out that tunnel and holding up that trophy at the end of the game, and knowing I'd already reached the greatest milestone."

The 31-25 victory over the Pittsburgh Steelers made Driver's mission complete. His legacy, already written with a rags-to-riches theme, now had some added meaning. He had joined select company at the top of his profession.

Driver made the first catch of the Super Bowl for the Packers, a full-speed, 24-yard reception over the middle to convert a third-and-9. After making the catch he sprung to his feet, amped, as he signaled first down. He was ready for this one.

Driver would catch just one more pass in the game, however, on a bittersweet evening in Arlington, Texas. Though he would be able to hoist the Lombardi Trophy

Driver hurts his ankle during second quarter action against the Steelers. *Photo by Jim Biever*

Although injured during the game, Driver did all he could from the sidelines to get the fans fired up.   *Photo by Jim Biever*

after the game, an ankle injury suffered in the second quarter would force him to the sideline where he could only watch.

But before that, Driver had intentions of returning to the game. During the extended halftime break, his ankle was taped up but his mobility and jumping ability was limited. So, he was ruled out by the team's medical personnel despite wanting to come back.

If the Packers needed any added motivation to win, they got it from Driver being out as well as veteran teammate Charles Woodson, who broke his collarbone in the second quarter.

Halftime soon took on a new meaning for the Packers: *We're not leaving here without getting a ring for these guys.*

They did just that. What injury and

pain took away, winning a championship cured.

"It's truly amazing. It's truly, truly a blessing," said Driver after the game. "This is something I've dreamed of for a long time and it's finally here. When that clock was ticking down, I didn't know what to do. I'm glad that I'm now able to say I am part of history." ∎

Top : Driver salutes the fans during the post Super Bowl celebration at Lambeau Field. *Photo by Jim Biever*

Middle: Driver showing off the Lombardi Trophy. *Photo by Jim Biever*

Left: Driver is interviewed following Super Bowl XLV. *Photo by Jim Biever*

Driver showing off his Super Bowl ring during the team's ring ceremony in June 2011. *AP Photo*

November 12, 2006
at Minnesota

After his 11-catch performance two years earlier, Driver continued to be a thorn in the Vikings' side with a career-high 191 receiving yards. Just before halftime, Driver caught a slant from Brett Favre, splitting the Vikings defense for an 82-yard touchdown. He finished the play in Bo Jackson-like fashion by running through end zone and up a tunnel underneath the stands.

Driver takes another hard hit across the middle but hangs on for the catch. *Photo by Jim Biever*

Driver out races Vikings safety Darren Sharper (42) to the end zone to complete a 82-yard touchdown during second quarter action. *AP Photo*

Photo by Jim Biever

Receivers came and receivers went but Donald Driver was the constant in Green Bay.

Even with a first-round pick used on Javon Walker in 2002, Driver was practically a one-man receiver corps for several seasons. From 2002 through 2007, Driver averaged 22.2 more receptions per season than the No. 2 wide receiver — and that's with Walker's team-high 89 catches in 2003.

When general manager Ted Thompson took over in 2005, one of his prime objectives was retooling the receiver corps, with Terrence Murphy (second round, 2005), Greg Jennings (second round, 2006), James Jones (third round, 2007) and Jordy Nelson (second round, 2008) added in four consecutive drafts.

With each season that passed, Driver was one year older and Jennings, Jones and Nelson got one year better.

Driver, as a proud man, proven veteran, team leader and fan favorite, could have raised a stink.

Instead, Driver stepped aside as gracefully as anyone could expect. He never complained. He didn't skip practice with phantom injuries. He went out and did like always did — put in an honest day's work and fought for opportunities based on merit rather than reputation.

"When I came in, I was the 13th guy down the totem pole and my goal was just to come in and work hard," Driver said. "When the guys slack, you've got to be the one to pull yourself together and go out there and make a play. That's what our group does. Every day you see these guys make plays and you're like, 'OK, I've got to make a play, too.' That's the ticket. We have a competition between us, and it's fun. There's no hard feelings. It's just go out there and make plays, and we laugh and joke about it in the locker room."

Driver and Jennings served as the No. 1/1-A receivers in 2008 and 2009. In 2010, Jennings became the marquee member of the group while Driver had his streak of 133 games with at least one catch snapped and finished with merely 51 receptions — his fewest since grabbing just 13 balls back in 2001.

Not once did Driver complain, and Driver's way spread to the rest of the receivers, who had be patient with only so many balls to go

Driver saw his playing time cut back in the 2012 season. He finished the year with 8 receptions for 77 yards and 2 touchdowns. *Photo by Jim Biever*

around in the Packers' deep offense.

"It starts from the top down," Jennings said. "When you have a guy like Donald who's been doing it for 52 years now, you can't come in and be that guy if you're watching the guy who's above you and he's not that way. It trickles down. It becomes a domino effect."

Then came the 2011 draft, when Thompson drafted Randall Cobb in the second round. Cobb wasn't just a receiver. He was taken to take Driver's place in the offense. Driver wouldn't have been the first player to give his successor the cold shoulder. Instead, Driver became a

Driver remained the ultimate teammate even as his playing time was reduced. Here he congratulates Chad Kuhn (30) after Kuhn scored a touchdown. *Photo by Jim Biever*

mentor and friend to the player he called "The Kid."

"'Drive' has been a blessing to me from the moment I walked through the doors of the Lambeau Field facilities," Cobb said. "I will cherish the locker- and meeting-room memories I was fortunate enough to have with him. I will always value the lessons he taught me on the field in showing me how and what

it takes to become a great receiver. But the things he taught me about life, as far as being a father, son, brother, role model and friend, will carry much more weight in my life both during and after my playing career. I'm thankful that the Lord crossed our paths and I can only hope and pray to have a career that he has had and make a difference in as many lives as he has."■

"He was a playmaker. That is the first thing that comes to my mind when I think of him on the field, all of the amazing catches he would make, the one-handed catches. He could just make plays. He would be practicing every single day, wouldn't take a day off no matter how many years he had been here. As far as a person and what he meant to this community, it speaks for itself with his foundation and all the things that he does and the way the fans love him. There is a reason why."

–Packers WR Jordy Nelson

"Obviously he is a great player, but I think he is an even better man. I think that is the starting point. It starts with the man, the person, and it all starts with that. I think everything he has been able to accomplish in his life, be it business, be it football, be it family, faith, I think it all starts with him as a man and what is in his heart. He did it the right way, he did it the Packer way, and it has been an honor to work with him during his journey."

–Packers wide receivers coach Edgar Bennett

Photo by Jim Biever

January 20, 2008, NFC Championship vs. New York Giants at Lambeau Field

Under brutally cold conditions, in a game where points were at a premium, Driver recorded the longest reception of his career, a 90-yarder from Brett Favre. Just after the snap, Driver successfully beat press coverage from Corey Webster by tossing the cornerback to the side. That allowed Favre to find him wide open at the 29-yard line. From there, he outraced three defenders the final 71 yards for the Packers first score of the game. Driver finished the game with five catches for a playoff-high 141 yards.

Above: Driver catches the Favre throw at the 29-yard line. *Photo by Jim Biever*

Opposite Page: Driver outruns three defenders the final 71-yards for the first score of the game. *Photo by Jim Biever*

Inset: Driver finishes the incredible play with a Lambeau Leap and then proceeds to blow the Packer faithful a kiss on the frigid evening. *Photos by Jim Biever*

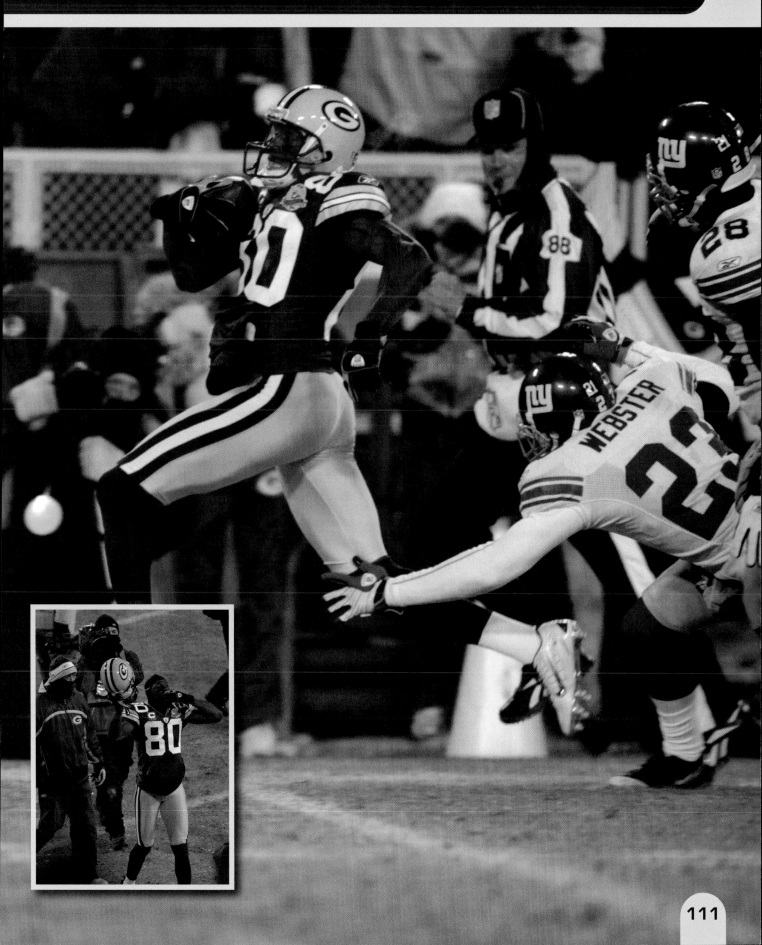

G iven his prolific numbers and rags-to-riches story, Donald Driver is one of the more beloved figures in Packers history.

Driver's charisma and personal story won over the rest of the nation, too, as he used his fancy footwork and indomitable work ethic to win Season 14 of ABC's "Dancing with the Stars" in May 2012.

"Amazing! Wow! This is awesome!" Driver exclaimed when his victory was announced.

A week later, Driver – his body fat reduced from 4 percent to 2 percent due to 10 or 11 hours per day of training – was back in Green Bay for offseason practices.

"It's good to see him back in his real uniform," coach Mike McCarthy joked.

A couple weeks after his dancing win and with Mirrorball Trophy in hand, Driver and his partner, professional dancer Peta Murgatroyd, were in Grand Chute, Wis., for Driver's annual charity softball game.

"I would've never expected this in a million years," Driver said. "When I walked in here in 1999, I would've never expected to have the fan base that I have now. I think you treat people like you want to be treated. I don't put myself on a pedestal, they do. And when they put me on that pedestal, I bring myself back down to earth, knowing I'm just a normal human being. I think now they see that. I think not just the Packers fans see that and Packer Nation sees

Driver and his Dancing With The Stars" parter Peta Murgatroyd dance on ABC's "Good Morning America" show in New York, May 2012. *AP Photo*

that, but the world sees that now, that I am a good guy, a great father, a great Christian man, and a great husband. And to me, that's what I wanted to show the world."

Driver and professional Murgatryod spent the entire season near the top of the leaderboard, thanks to the votes of Packer Nation combined with the three judges' consistently strong scores. In the finale, they edged out opera singer Katherine Jenkins and Latin star William Levy.

"He's the best celebrity dance partner anyone could ask for," Murgatroyd, a first-time winner, said. "I was lucky."

For their final dance, Driver and Murgatryod received a perfect 30 for their freestyle dance to Cowboy Troy's "I Play Chicken with the Train."

"For me, it did feel like the Super Bowl because I was giving Peta something that she dreamed of for a long time, and that's winning that mirror ball," Driver said. "For a pro dancer, that's the greatest milestone you can reach, and for me, I'm just glad I gave it to her. So, at the end of the day, it was amazing."

Driver, Hall of Fame running back Emmitt Smith and retired receiver Hines Ward are the three football players to have won the Mirrorball Trophy.

"It's another chapter in the book, I guess you could say," Driver said.

Driver and dance partner, Peta Murgatroyd, appear with the Mirrorball Trophy on ABC's "Good Morning America" show in May 2012.
AP Photo

"People on the street, people that never watched the show before, now they know who I am. Even when I left New York, people were in the airport like, 'You're that guy that just won "Dancing with the Stars."' But I'm like, 'I do play football.' They're like, 'Yeah, no one cares about you playing football. But everyone does care about Dancing with the Stars.'"■

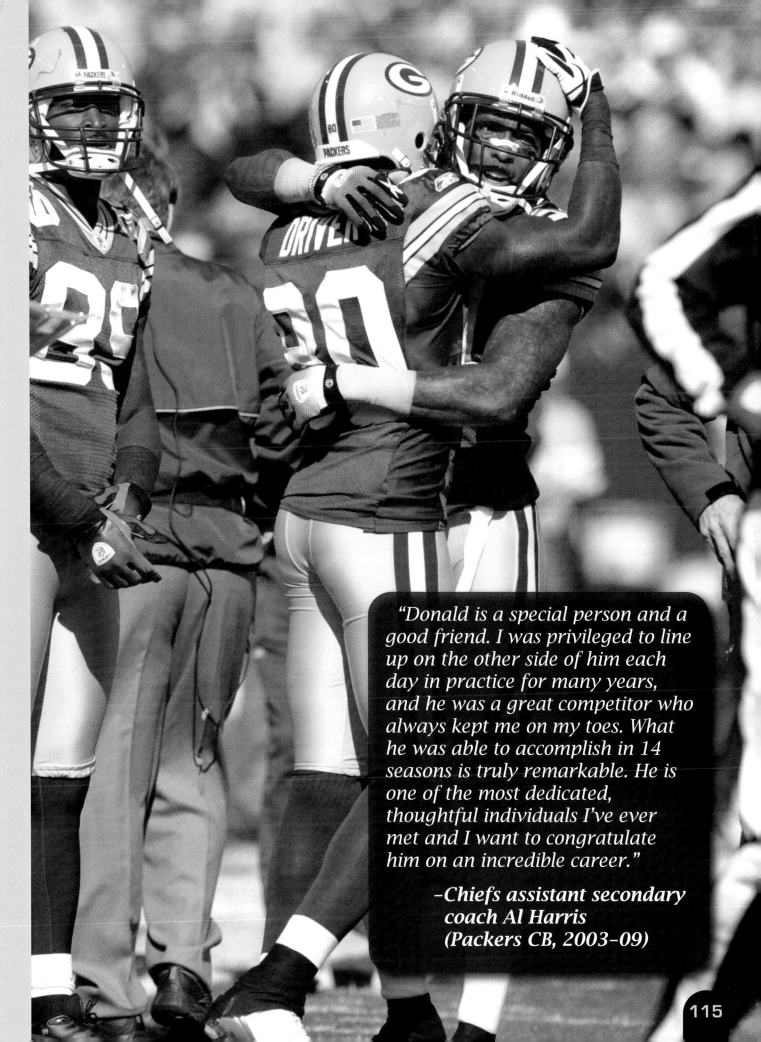

"Donald is a special person and a good friend. I was privileged to line up on the other side of him each day in practice for many years, and he was a great competitor who always kept me on my toes. What he was able to accomplish in 14 seasons is truly remarkable. He is one of the most dedicated, thoughtful individuals I've ever met and I want to congratulate him on an incredible career."

–Chiefs assistant secondary coach Al Harris (Packers CB, 2003–09)

September 27, 2009
at St. Louis

Driver had made difficult catches in practice look routine before. But among his one-handed grabs in game action, this one might have been his best. Streaking down the left sideline, Driver managed to haul in, with just his left hand, a long throw from Aaron Rodgers while cornerback Bradley Fletcher held his right arm. Fletcher was penalized on the play for pass interference, but the Packers declined because the spectacular play resulted in a 46-yard gain.

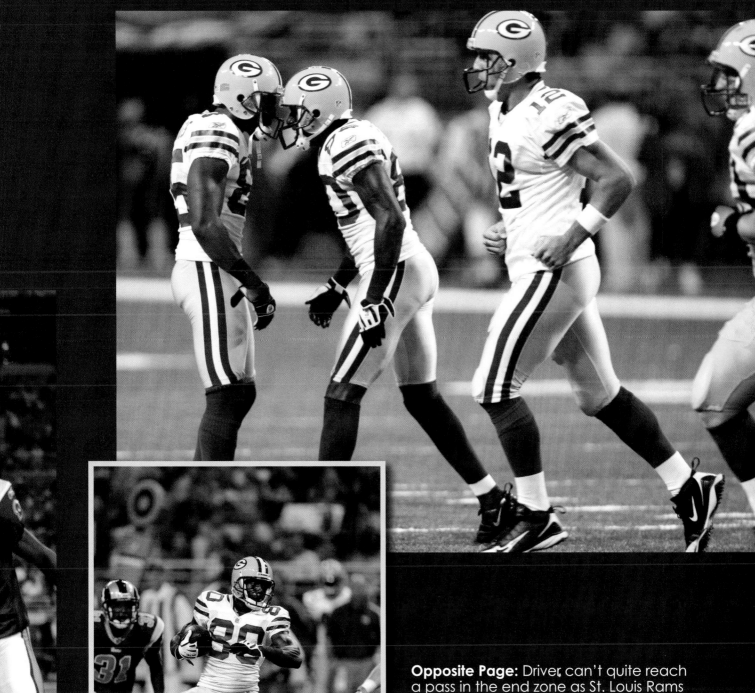

Opposite Page: Driver, can't quite reach a pass in the end zone as St. Louis Rams cornerback Justin King looks on during the first quarter. *AP Photo*

Above: Packers wide receiver Greg Jennings celebrates with Driver after a touchdown during the second quarter. *AP Photo*

Left: Driver makes a move after the reception. *AP Photo*

Green Bay Packers' Donald Driver, left, and Greg Jennings run a drill during training camp in 2011.
AP Photo

When Goodwill forged a relationship with Donald Driver, it unveiled the slogan, "Believe in the power of work."

There could have been no better spokesman than Driver, the self-made superstar.

"That's me all the way," Driver said before the 2010 season. "I think that's why they allowed me to be a part of

their family is because I believe in what they believe. I believe hard work pays off. My thing was, when everyone else was sleeping, I was still working. To this day, I still believe that."

That hard work allowed Driver to remake his body, with an additional 20 pounds of muscle allowing him to survive the rigors as one of the league's premier over-the-middle receiver threats. From 2004 through 2009 – spanning ages 29 to 34– Driver had six consecutive 1,000-yard seasons. Only four receivers had more yards during that time.

"As I get up in age, I have to work more than the young guys that I have in my receiving group," Driver said. "They're young, they have a bright future and I feel like I have to continue to prove myself. I think year in and year out, no one has ever put me on top of a pedestal, and I don't care for that. I don't care to be up there. When I play the game, I play at a high level. Every year, I feel like I have to prove myself, regardless of whether it was when I came in 1999 or I'm here in 2010. I still have to prove myself as being one of the best receivers in the National Football League. That's what I have to do, and when it's all said and done, I'm hoping that someone would give me the credit and say he was one of the best players ever."

To the end, Driver was a marvel. With his age and accomplishments, Driver could have taken a day off here and there in training camp or maybe loafed through a couple of drills. Instead, Driver attacked every day as if he were still that seventh-round long shot out of Alcorn State.

In other words, he believed in the power of work.

"The way he goes about his business, the guy never misses practice," receiver Jordy Nelson said. "I know if I was in the league 10, 11 years, I'd be thinking, 'I'm taking this practice off. I've done enough reps.' But he's out there every day. Off the field, just a great guy, family man and it's been fun playing with him, that's for sure."

"Donald, he conducts himself the right way," quarterback Aaron Rodgers added. "I think the first thing that you really appreciate about Donald is he practices every day and hard. He works hard and he's a leader through the way he practices, which is very important for team chemistry and for the young guys he mentors."

As the established star on the receiver corps, Driver took that mentorship role seriously. He made the others feel welcome — he quickly labeled a 6-foot-4 undrafted rookie named Tori Gurley "Slinkie," for instance. By doing things the right way, Driver fostered a cooperative spirit in which no individual was bigger than the receiver group as a whole.

"Donald who?" asked fellow receiver James Jones. "Oh, him? Seriously: Hard worker. My first impression of him was hard worker. He's earned everything he's got. It's a tribute to his hard work. Everything he has, he deserves." ■

December 5, 2010, vs. San Francisco 49ers at Lambeau Field

Aaron Rodgers called it one of the most exciting plays he's ever been a part of. Mike McCarthy said he'll never forget it. And for the collective masses, it's the play that best illustrates what Driver is all about. After getting free behind the 49ers' zone coverage, Driver completed a 61-yard touchdown by forcing three missed tackles before three more defenders converged on him inside the 5-yard line. By then it was too late. An exhausted Driver, who racked up 38 yards after the catch on the play, had already crossed the goal line. "It kind of worked out in my favor because they jumped Greg Jennings and they left me wide open," said Driver. "After that, I just said I wasn't going to be denied. I wanted to get to the end zone. To shake off all those tackles and for Drew (Andrew Quarless) to make a block after that, and then it was just me trying to carry the rest to the end zone. I have to say if I look at one play of my career that stands alone, that's the best one of my career."

Opposite: Driver prepares to break the tackle of the Niners' Nate Clements (22). Dashon Goldson (38) gives chase. *Photo by Jim Biever*

Right: Nick Collins embraces Driver after his 61-yard touchdown play. *Photo by Jim Biever*

On February 6, 2013 the Green Bay Packers held a special ceremony in the Atrium at Lambeau Field – the retirement of #80 Donald Driver. Never before had the Packers organization held a public retirement ceremony. Never before had a Packer been as beloved by the fans as Driver had. More than 1,000 lucky fans were granted access to the hour-long event to say farewell to their hero. Packers president Mark Murphy spoke, as well as General Manager Ted Thompson. Head Coach Mike McCarthy praised Driver's work ethic. Even Governor Scott Walker got in the act declaring it "Donald Driver Day" throughout Wisconsin. Finally, it was Driver's turn to address the crowd. Below is the full transcript of his speech:

"I told myself that I wasn't going to cry today so I'm going to try to hold all the emotions back as much as possible. But I have to say this, that I love you all so much. You guys stood out in the cold to get tickets to share this moment with me. You all are crazy. But now you know why Packer fans are so special because they show the loyalty. They show the respect. So now, I give you all the respect."

"First, I would like to thank God for allowing me to be here. It has been a blessing to have the ability to play this game, to be able to see the love, the joy, the dedication that we see in others. Jesus Christ has given me the wisdom to understand when things must come to an end. Sometimes, I ask myself, 'Why now?' But God says he will make a way out of no way to make

Driver speaks during his retirement ceremony Wednesday, Feb. 6, 2013, at Lambeau Field. *AP Photo*

Driver listens as Packers head coach Mike McCarthy speaksd during Drivers' retirement ceremony at Lambeau Field.   *AP Photo*

you understand the reason why. So today is the day that I have decided to retire from the National Football League. It has been a tough decision. But my family and I felt it was time for the next chapter in our lives. Now, who knows what that may be. But my wife already made it clear that the first thing in retirement is getting the squirrels out of our attic in Dallas. So that's the first thing I'll be doing when I get back."

"You know, even though I feel that I can still play the game, God has made the answer clear to me. Retirement is now. I have to retire as a Green Bay Packer."

"I've always said that I never want to wear another uniform – but always the green and gold. Sometimes, I sit at home and think about the history of this great franchise and I think of the players and the great coaches that came before me like Vince Lombardi, Bart Starr, Ray Nitschke, Willie Davis, Jerry Kramer, the great Reggie White, Brett Favre, James Lofton, Sterling Sharpe, Ahman Green, Rob Davis, I mean this list goes on and on and on. So I felt that this is an opportunity to walk away from the game knowing that I've given it all that I can."

With his wife Betina and daughter Charity at his side, Driver waves to fans during his retirement ceremony at Lambeau Field. *AP Photo*

"So I owe it to the fans and to this fine organization not to tarnish the legacy that they have established in me and my family."

"So now my list goes to thanking people. I have to thank the man who brought me here. He can't be here today but I talked to him on the phone and he said, 'it's an honor to know you, to be a part of your life.' But I told Ron I could not have done it without him believing in me. So I'd like to thank Ron Wolf. I would like to thank this man who became a father figure to me. He always opened his doors to allow me to walk in if I had something to talk about. But he retired on me too soon – Bob Harlan. I have to thank one of my good friends. We've been together since '99. He left me and came back. It's an honor to play for Coach Mike McCarthy. I know where this team is going, but I love you. I really do."

The man that don't talk too much and plays the poker face. I love this guy. He doesn't get emotonal for anything, the great Ted Thompson.

Over the years I got a chance to know you well and your family. I think what you've done for this organization and what you're going to continue to do for this

Fans hold up a sign in support for Driver during his retirement ceremony at Lambeau Field.
AP Photo

organization is truly a blessing. We're glad to have you as our president.

I have to thank all of my head coaches: Mike Sherman, Ray Rhodes. My position coaches, Ray Sherman, Charlie Baggett, James Franklin, Jimmy Robinson and the great Edgar Bennett, aka EB. And the man, I don't know if he's here, but the man who came down to Alcorn State and saw this little skinny kid, like everyone said, and he worked me out and he told Ron Wolf, 'This guy is something special' and he told Ted, 'This guy is something speical.' I have to thank the guy who came and worked me out. Alonzo, I don't know if you're here but Alonzo Highsmith, I love you. Thank you.

I have to thank the entire Green Bay Packers organization. I have to thank the Board of Directors, the trainers, the equipment staff, the weight room staff, the community relations, PR, marketing, ticket office, security, Pro Shop, financial department. I love you guys, really. Thank you, all, for everything.

I would like to thank my teammates, past and present. It's been an honor to wear the green and gold with you guys. To my family, to my friends and to all of my partners, thank you for the great relationships. The one person I have to thank truly for putting me out there in the community – he's a good friend of mine, Brian Lammi. To my mothers... thank you for always loving me and supporting me and always needing me when we need you, even if it's on short notice to come babysit the kids, I thank you for it. To my mom, thank you for the love, for instilling in me to always follow my dreams. I love you for that.

To my grandparents – they cannot be here – I love you guys. And to my dad, he can't be here today because he's fighting lung cancer. I love him to death. I thank him for allowing me to be the man that I am today. To my babies, Cristian, Christina and Charity, Daddy loves you guys. Thank you for always being my No. 1 cheering section, even though you guys have never watched your Daddy play a full game because you're always in the hallway having your own. Daddy loves you. And to my better half, the love of my life: Baby, I love you. I thank you for the love, the support for the last 16 years of our life, the 14 years of playing this game and the 13 years of marriage. I've said it before, you're the back bone of our family. Life is what it is and life is whatever it may be, but life without you in my life is nothing. I love you.

Last, but not least, to the fans. I want to thank you all for the love, the joy, the cheers, the ups and though we haven't given you too many downs. This day is not just for me, this day is for you. Twelve years ago, I signed my first big contract for the Green Bay Packers and I promised you all that I would never wear another uniform. So today, we make that official. I keep my promise to you. The loyalty you all have instiled in me and my family, I have to keep my loyalty to you and not play for another team and to retire in the green and gold. I love you all, take care and God bless.

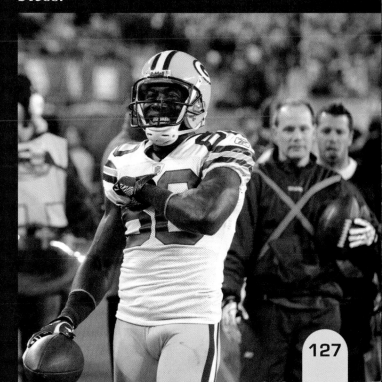

DRIVER BY THE NUMBERS

WR DONALD DRIVER 1999-2012

A look at where Driver ranks in franchise history in several categories:

Player Receptions
1. Donald Driver, 1999-2012 743
2. Sterling Sharpe, 1988-94 595
3. James Lofton, 1978-86 530

Player Receiving Yards
1. Donald Driver, 1999-2012 10,137
2. James Lofton, 1978-86 9,656
3. Sterling Sharpe, 1988-94 8,134

Player 1,000-Yard Seasons
1. Donald Driver, 1999-2012 7
2t. James Lofton, 1978-86 5
2t. Sterling Sharpe, 1988-94 5

Player 100-Yard Games
1. James Lofton, 1978-86 32
2. Sterling Sharpe, 1988-94 29
3. Don Hutson, 1935-45 24
4. Greg Jennings, 2006-12 23
5. Donald Driver, 1999-2012 22

Player TD Catches
1. Don Hutson, 1935-45 99
2. Sterling Sharpe, 1988-94 65
3. Donald Driver, 1999-2012 61

Player Games Played
1. Brett Favre, 1992-2007 255
2. Donald Driver, 1999-2012 205
3. Bart Starr, 1956-71 196

Player Yards From Scrimmage
1. Ahman Green, 2000-06, 2009 11,048
2. Donald Driver, 1999-2012 10,354
3. James Lofton, 1978-86 9,901

Player 50-Catch Seasons
1. Donald Driver, 1999-2012 9
2t. James Lofton, 1978-86 7
2t. Sterling Sharpe, 1988-94 7

Player Consec. Games/Reception
1. Donald Driver, 2001-10 133
2. Sterling Sharpe, 1988-94 103
3. Edgar Bennett, 1993-96 60

CAREER STATS

Year	GP	GS	No	Yds	Avg	Lg	TD
1999	6	0	3	31	10.3	12	1
2000	16	2	21	322	15.3	49	1
2001	13	2	13	167	12.8	37	1
2002	16	16	70	1,064	15.2	85t	9
2003	15	15	52	621	11.9	41	2
2004	16	11	84	1,208	14.4	50	9
2005	16	16	86	1,221	14.2	59	5
2006	16	16	92	1,295	14.1	82t	8
2007	15	14	82	1,048	12.8	47	2
2008	16	16	74	1,012	13.7	71t	5
2009	16	16	70	1,061	15.2	71t	6
2010	15	15	51	565	11.1	61t	4
2011	16	15	37	445	12.0	35t	6
2012	13	1	8	77	9.6	26t	2
Total	205	155	743	10,137	13.6	85t	61